D0743209

North American

INDIAN NATIONS

NATIVE PEOPLES
of
CALIFORNIA

Linda Lowery

LERNER PUBLICATIONS ◆ MINNEAPOLIS

The editors would like to note that we have made every effort to work with consultants from various nations, as well as fact-checkers, to ensure that the content in this series is accurate and appropriate. In addition to this title, we encourage readers to seek out content produced by the nations themselves online and in print.

Consultant: Jill Norwood, Community Services Specialist, National Museum of the American Indian (Tolowa/Yurok/Karuk)

Lerner Publications Company
A division of Lerner Publishing Group, Inc.
241 First Avenue North
Minneapolis, MN 55401 USA

For reading levels and more information, look up this title at www.lernerbooks.com.

Main body text set in Rockwell Std Light 12/16.
Typeface provided by Monotype Typography.

Library of Congress Cataloging-in-Publication Data

Lowery, Linda, 1949–
    Native peoples of California / by Linda Lowery.
        pages cm. — (North American Indian nations)
    Audience: Grades 4–6.
    ISBN 978-1-4677-7932-6 (lb : alk. paper) — ISBN 978-1-4677-8321-7 (pb : alk. paper) — ISBN 978-1-4677-8322-4 (eb pdf)
    1. Indians of North America—California—Juvenile literature. I. Title.
E78.C15L68 2015
979.4004'97—dc23   2015001958

Manufactured in the United States of America
1 – PC – 7/15/16

CONTENTS

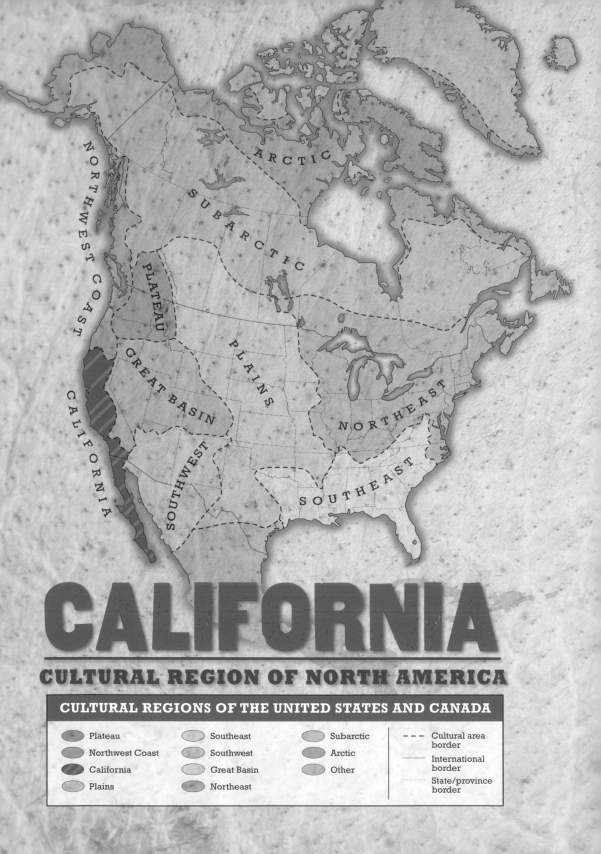

ARCTIC

SUBARCTIC

NORTHWEST COAST

PLATEAU

CALIFORNIA

GREAT BASIN

PLAINS

NORTHEAST

SOUTHWEST

SOUTHEAST

CALIFORNIA
CULTURAL REGION OF NORTH AMERICA

CULTURAL REGIONS OF THE UNITED STATES AND CANADA

- Plateau
- Northwest Coast
- California
- Plains
- Southeast
- Southwest
- Great Basin
- Northeast
- Subarctic
- Arctic
- Other
- - - - Cultural area border
- International border
- State/province border

INTRODUCTION

In the beginning, water covered the world. Old Man Coyote asked Frog to dive down and bring him some mud from the ocean floor. With the mud, Coyote made land, and animals came. But there were no people. Old Man Coyote walked across the land he had made. Everywhere he wanted people to live, he stuck two sticks in the ground. The sticks became human beings. That is how the world was created.

The Miwok (MEE-wahk) people of California tell this story of the beginning of their people. California is home to many American Indian cultural groups. Each group has its own creation story, its own history, and its own way of life.

Early California peoples communicated with one another about their cultural traditions, events, and everyday life through talking and storytelling. They also shared information by making carvings, singing, and drawing.

Origins
Scholars believe that California Indian cultures may be the oldest living cultures in North America. Archaeologists have found a thirteen-thousand-year-old skeleton on an island where the Chumash (CHEW-mosh)

PEOPLES OF CALIFORNIA

The California cultural region was the traditional home of many American Indian nations. This map shows the areas where some of them lived before Europeans arrived in the region.

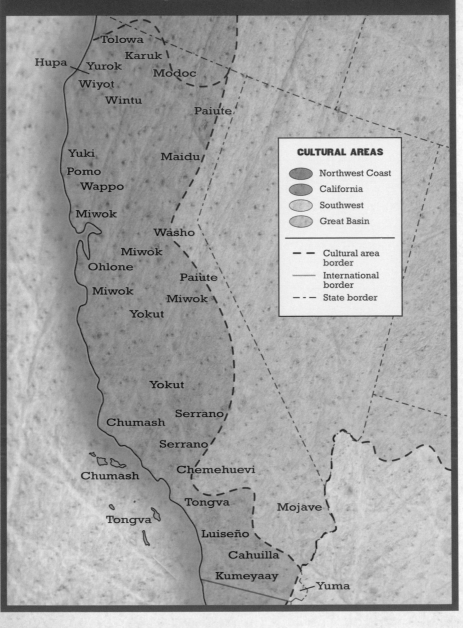

CULTURAL AREAS

- Northwest Coast
- California
- Southwest
- Great Basin

– – Cultural area border
— International border
–·– State border

Tolowa
Karuk
Hupa
Yurok
Modoc
Wiyot
Wintu
Paiute
Yuki
Maidu
Pomo
Wappo
Miwok
Washo
Miwok
Ohlone
Paiute
Miwok
Miwok
Yokut
Yokut
Serrano
Chumash
Serrano
Chumash
Chemehuevi
Tongva
Mojave
Tongva
Luiseño
Cahuilla
Kumeyaay
Yuma

settled. Some believe
the earliest settlers
came from Asia.
Nomadic hunters may
have crossed a land
bridge to North America
and gradually moved
south. One theory is that
early American Indians
traveled down the
Pacific coast by boat.

Many California Indians settled along the Pacific coast.

California peoples
have their own beliefs
about their origins.
Many California Indians
believe their ancestors have always lived in the region.
However they arrived, American Indians spread out across
what would later become California. Their homes stretched
from the Sierra Nevada in the east to the Pacific coast in the
west. Redwood and fir forests covered the northwestern part
of the region. The Mojave Desert spanned the southeast. In
the middle was a vast area of woods and grasslands, later
called the Central Valley. Each group of people adapted to the
area where they lived.

Many Miwok groups settled in the Central Valley. Other
Miwok groups lived near the Washo (WAH-show) people in
the mountains. Some groups, including the Modoc (MOH-doc),
lived at the most northern point of what became California. The
Hupa (HOO-puh), the Pomo (POH-moh), the Tolowa (TAHL-ah-
wah), the Yuki (YOO-kee), and the Wiyot (WEE-yot) lived on
the northern coast by the Pacific Ocean. The Chumash and the

Tongva (TONG-vah, also called Gabrielino or Gabrieleño) settled farther south along the Pacific and the islands off the coast.

Many Peoples

California Indians had many things in common. But the region's landscape kept different groups apart. Communities were spread out, with few nearby neighbors. Mountain ranges and dry desert lands could make long-distance travel difficult. Since groups lived separately, they developed different ways of life. They spoke nearly one hundred languages from six main language groups. A single language could also have different versions, or dialects. Members of each cultural group generally spoke the same language and shared many other traits.

By the time European explorers arrived in the 1500s, California was home to more than three hundred thousand American Indians. There may have been as many as one million. Explorers reported that they met five hundred distinct cultural groups.

After California Indians came into contact with Europeans, their lives began to change dramatically. Spain claimed California as part of its empire. Later, Mexico took control of the region. In 1850, California became part of the United States. Every change in power affected California Indians.

Europeans carried germs that were new to the California Indians. Thousands died from contagious diseases such as smallpox and measles. Thousands more died from starvation or in violent conflict with Europeans.

By 1900, only about fifteen thousand California Indians were left alive. Some groups were gone, with no survivors. Most had been driven off their lands and forced onto reservations. Despite this, most California Indian groups have survived into the

LANGUAGE FAMILIES OF CALIFORNIA PEOPLES

LANGUAGE FAMILY	MAJOR CULTURAL GROUPS
Algic	Wiyot, Yurok
Athabascan	Hupa, Tolowa
Hokan	Chumash, Karuk, Kumeyaay (also called Diegueño), Mojave, Pomo, Washo, Yuma
Penutian	Maidu, Miwok, Modoc, Ohlone, Wintun, Yokut
Uto-Aztecan	Cahuilla, Chemehuevi, Paiute, Luiseño, Serrano, Tongva
Yukian	Yuki, Wappo

twenty-first century. Many have gradually begun to thrive again. They have set up their own governments and businesses. They teach their children traditional skills and spiritual beliefs, and they hold ceremonies to celebrate their heritage. Languages, poetry, songs, dances, dressmaking, basketmaking, and canoeing are among the many traditions that California peoples still practice and pass on.

CHAPTER 1

LAND OF
PLENTY

These days, California Indians live in the same kinds of homes, shop at the same kinds of stores, and wear the same kinds of clothes as most other Americans. But in California's early history, the area's native peoples lived in more traditional ways. Early California was a land brimming with natural riches. In the lush northwestern part of the region, groups settled along rivers, lagoons, and bays. The northeast was mountainous, while desert covered the southeast. The region's Central Valley had grasslands, wetlands, and woods. Each area's natural resources helped shape the lives and traditions of the peoples who lived there.

Homes

California Indians used the natural resources that surrounded them to build their shelters. The Tolowa made square-shaped houses from redwood planks. Rectangular Hupa houses were made from cedar. Each Hupa home had a fire pit in the middle for heat and cooking. The Miwok lived in cone-shaped homes, made of bark or wood from pine or cedar trees and covered

Many traditional Hupa dwellings, such as this one, were built in valleys and made of cedar planks.

with packed earth. A Cahuilla (kah-WEE-ah) home, called a *kish,* was covered with reeds and brush. Other cultures in the Central Valley used deerskins to cover the frames of their homes. The Washo covered their homes in deerskin or antelope skin.

Farther south along the coast, the Chumash bent willow poles to build huge dome-shaped homes. These structures were covered with woven mats, often made from a plant called tule. Inside, the space was divided into rooms with ladders to reach built-in platform beds. Some shelters on islands off the coast were made of whalebone. In the far southeast, the Yuma (YOO-mah) built homes with branches and bushes and covered them with mud or sand to stay cool. Yuma homes were square-shaped and about 20 feet (6 meters) wide. Sometimes other California Indians built dwellings three times that size that could fit several families. Kumeyaay (KOOM-yahy) homes, called *ewaas,* were built with willow branches and covered with tule. People placed stones around the outside of the house to keep animals away and to help block the wind.

Some groups had both winter homes and summer homes, so they lived comfortably when the weather changed. For example, in the southern desert, the Mojave (moh-HAHV-ay) built airy, one-sided homes for summer. In winter, they lived in sturdier, thatch-covered structures.

Food

California Indians had three main ways of getting food: farming, hunting or fishing, and gathering. Most groups hunted animals that lived in their areas. Groups that lived along the coast or near rivers fished. People also gathered nuts, berries, and fruit that grew nearby. Edible plants grew everywhere, even in the desert. Acorns were a basic food for many groups. Women ground acorns into flour or paste to make soup and bread.

Northwestern groups hunted deer, caught fish, and gathered acorns. For instance, the Karuk (kah-ROOK) fished for salmon and trout and hunted deer and elk. In the fall, the Tolowa left their coastal villages to gather acorns and catch fish in the rivers. Interior groups hunted rabbit and deer and gathered acorns, seeds, and grasses. For example, the Miwok collected mushrooms and berries, which they crushed, dried, and made into cider.

The ocean, bays, and wetlands of the southern coast provided seaweed, eel, fish, shellfish, whales, and seabirds. In the southern desert, groups such as the Cahuilla hunted bighorn sheep in addition to gathering plants. Southeastern desert dwellers near modern-day Arizona hunted rabbits, birds, and wild pigs called javelinas (ha-vuh-LEE-nahs). People fished in mountain streams and gathered cactus,

ACORNS

Acorns grow on many varieties of oak trees in California. Depending on the type of oak tree, an acorn shell can be smooth, scaly, hairy, pointy, dark brown, light tan, or striped. Most California Indians valued acorns as a major food source. To prepare acorns for eating, women removed the nuts from the shell. Then they smashed and ground the nuts using a stone tool called a *mano.* Finally, they soaked the ground acorns to remove their bitter flavor. This acorn flour was used to make soup, mush, or bread. Extra food was stored in small structures made of willow tree branches. Willow contains a natural insect repellent, so any stored food stayed bug-free.

seeds, and fruits. They also gathered tule and ate the bulbs of its roots. Unlike most California groups, the desert groups farmed too. They mostly planted corn and beans along the Colorado River.

Tools

California Indians used a variety of baskets to carry and store food, water, and other important items. Some baskets were so tightly woven that they could hold water without leaking. In dry areas with little rain, storing water was especially important.

FOOD SOURCES OF EARLY CALIFORNIA PEOPLES

PEOPLE	LOCATION	MAJOR FOOD SOURCES
Cahuilla	Southeastern desert	Hunting: rabbits, deer, bighorn sheep Gathering: acorns, agaves, cactus roots, pine nuts, mesquite beans, dates from palm trees
Kumeyaay	Southwestern coast	Hunting: deer, sheep, antelope, doves, geese, quail, rabbits, squirrels Fishing: fish, octopus Gathering: acorns, bird eggs, clams
Maidu	Central Valley	Fishing: salmon, trout, eel Hunting: deer, elk, antelope Gathering: acorns, pine nuts, roots, insects
Modoc	Northwestern coast	Fishing: salmon, trout Hunting: antelope, rabbits Gathering: roots, greens, fruit
Mojave	Southeastern desert	Farming: beans, corn, pumpkins Hunting: rabbits and beaver Gathering: mesquite beans
Wiyot	Northwestern coast	Fishing: salmon and other fish, sea lions Hunting: deer, elk Gathering: berries

Other baskets were sturdy enough to use for cooking food over hot stones.

Pottery was also useful for storage and cooking. Desert peoples such as the Mojave and the Kumeyaay used clay to make pots and dishes. The Chumash carved pots from soapstone

The Karuk made baskets for a variety of tasks, such as cooking and holding water.

that they mined on nearby Santa Catalina Island. Wood and animal bones could also be made into dishes. The Hupa used elk antlers to make spoons.

Bows and arrows were common hunting tools. The Cahuilla made bows and arrows out of wood from local willow and mesquite trees. People used spears and nets to fish. Miwok fishing spears had obsidian points. Fishing nets were woven from plant fiber.

Members of fishing cultures built boats. Redwood canoes were common, especially among northern groups such as the Tolowa, the Yurok (YER-ock), and the Wiyot. The Yurok used a stone-handled tool made of mussel shell to dig out huge logs. The canoes were sometimes 30 feet (9 m) long. From these canoes, people caught fish, mollusks, and sea lions.

Coastal groups made tools from whalebone or shells. In the Central Valley, fishing and hunting tools were made from wood, rocks, and plants in the area. In the northeast part of the region, volcanic mountains supplied people with obsidian, which was carved into arrowheads and knives. Obsidian was also used for trade.

Trade

Since the weather was usually mild, California Indians were able to travel often. If they went by ocean or river, they mostly traveled in canoes. Traders exchanged resources with other California Indians and then returned to their villages. Trading allowed many California groups to use items that they could not get in their own areas. Seashells, feathers, whalebone tools, and black obsidian rocks were popular trade items.

California peoples had many forms of money. The Chumash and Wappo used clamshells. The shells were shaped, polished, hung on strings, and worn around their necks. Among northern California peoples, dentalia (den-TAY-lee-ah) were the most important unit of money. Dentalia are mollusk shells that are shaped like a tiny elephant tusk. One

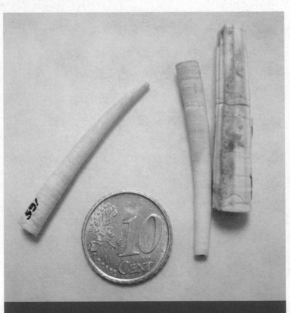

Dentalia were considered an important form of currency for many California cultures. They are shown here beside a ten-cent euro coin.

TRAVELING BY WATER

CULTURAL GROUP	LOCATION	WATER VEHICLE
Chumash	Southwestern coast	*Tomols* (large canoes powered by double-paddle oars)
Modoc	Northwestern coast	Redwood dugout canoes
Mojave	Southeastern desert	Rafts built from reeds or logs
Yokut	Central Valley	Balsas (rafts made from bundles of tied cattails, tule, or brush)
Yurok	Northwestern coast	Balsas and cedar dugout canoes

string of fine dentalia was worth the price of a redwood dugout canoe. The Yurok and the Hupa stored their dentalia in purses made from elk antlers and seashells. In some groups, dentalia were made into jewelry and worn as a sign of wealth.

Clothing

When the weather was mild, California peoples did not need much clothing. They often went barefoot, wearing shoes only when it was raining, cold, or very hot. Many desert women wore sandals of woven yucca fibers. Along the coast, some groups used tule. The Cahuilla made sandals from agave fiber. Other groups, including the Luiseño (loo-SEN-yoh), made sandals from yucca and moccasins from animal skin.

Many American Indian women of the California desert regions wore sandals made of yucca fibers.

In warm weather, men wore very little clothing. Some men wore breechcloths made of animal skin or tule. In the Central Valley, people used deerskin for their clothes. Desert women wore aprons made of tree bark. Women on the northwest coast made skirts from sea grass and feathers. In the north, women often wore aprons and skirts made from cedar bark. Hupa women made dresses from yucca and attached shells for decoration.

California winters could be cold, even in the desert. The Mojave and the Yuma made animal skins into robes and blankets. Coastal groups added warmth by attaching feathers, rabbit fur, and sea otter skins to clothing. They also wore robes made of animal skins. Very wealthy Miwok women wore capes made of feathers.

For ceremonies, California Indians wore decorative clothing. In the north, mink fur was used to make hair ties. People sewed clamshells, dentalia, abalone shells, and pine nuts to dresses for dancing. Many groups eventually traded with Europeans for bells, beads, and thimbles. The Hupa made headdresses of owl and woodpecker feathers. These decorative items are still worn on ceremonial clothing.

Tattooing was also common, especially for women. Different designs could show things such as a person's nation or family ties. Hupa and Yurok men had arm tattoos. They used these tattoos to measure the sizes of shells for trading. (Bigger shells were more valuable.) Yurok women got tattoos on their chins every five years to mark their age. Among other groups, such as the Yurok, women commonly got chin tattoos when they reached adulthood.

CHAPTER 2

BELIEFS AND
PRACTICES

In many California cultures, men and women had separate jobs. Often men did the hunting and fishing, while women gathered plants and prepared food. Among the Wiyot, both men and women hunted. Mojave men and women shared many tasks. For instance, men planted crops, and women harvested them. Mojave men and women also worked together to make pottery. Though their roles varied, men and women both honored and passed down the traditions and beliefs that made their cultures unique.

Family and Community

California Indians lived in villages. Many villages had two locations: one for the summer and one for the winter. These communities varied in size. Some desert communities had as few as fifty people. Some thriving Chumash villages had up to a thousand people.

Cultures had different ways of organizing their villages. Usually a village had a roundhouse, a central structure large enough for big meetings and ceremonial dances. Sweat lodges for spiritual ceremonies were also important buildings. A Tolowa village was split up into areas for homes, work, and burials. A Pomo village had a roundhouse and a sweat lodge in the middle. Family homes surrounded these central buildings. Several generations of the same family sometimes lived together.

In many cultures, especially in the southern part of California, people belonged to clans—groups of related families. Clan members often shared rights to property or worked together during hunts and harvests. Among some cultural groups, clan members lived together in the same village. This was true of the Cahuilla, the Luiseño, the Kumeyaay, and the Serrano (ser-RAHN-oh). In other cultures, such as the Mojave and the Yuma, clan members were scattered across different villages. Clans' names were often connected to animals they honored. For example, the Chumash have a Dolphin clan, and the Yokut (YOH-kuht) have a bear clan.

The roundhouse was a community building in many California Indian villages. It usually stood in the middle of a village, and family homes were built around it.

Leadership

Most villages were self-governing. Local leaders were in charge of each community's needs. Villages in the same cultural group might trade with one another and share family ties. Often nearby villages worked together for celebrations, ceremonies, or defense against common enemies.

Many village chiefs were born into a family of leaders. In northwestern groups, such as the Hupa and the Tolowa, a village's richest man often served as the chief. Each Chumash village had a leader, a *wot,* who could be a man or a woman. A Cahuilla village leader, a *net,* was always a man.

Village chiefs had many duties. For instance, Yokut chiefs helped care for the poor, met with visitors, and organized ceremonies. A Miwok chief managed the acorn harvest, took care of ceremonies, and held meetings in the roundhouse. Modoc villages had two leaders. One chief handled everyday matters, and one chief made military decisions.

Healers were important spiritual leaders. Sometimes they held more power than chiefs.

Healers sometimes used rattles as a part of their treatments. This rattle once belonged to a healer and is made of silk moth cocoons.

THE SPIRIT WORLD

Native California traditions say that all things have spirits, including animals, trees, rocks, water, wind, and air. Spirits have great power. They can help people, but they also can cause trouble. The Tongva, for example, tell a legend about seven turtles that hold up the land to keep it from sinking. This is very helpful to people. When the turtles swim in different directions, however, they can cause earthquakes.

Among the Kumeyaay, both women and men could be spiritual leaders. In other groups, such as the Modoc, healers were usually men. Healers used prayer and medical skills to help sick and injured people. A healer often gathered and prepared herbs that could treat illnesses and injuries. Kumeyaay tea, made with willow bark, cured headaches. Groups including the Miwok and the Chumash used the nettle plant to soothe pain. Healers also conducted ceremonies to heal sick people.

Ceremonies

Life for early California Indians was shaped by the seasons. Each spring or summer, salmon leave their ocean habitats and migrate upriver. This salmon run was the best fishing time for northern coastal peoples. Groups such as the Tolowa and the Yurok held a first salmon ceremony to give thanks for this important food source.

Every fall, communities held acorn harvests. For example, the Kumeyaay left their villages and camped in the mountains

During the salmon run, many salmon leap out of the water to swim upstream. This made them an easy target for California Indian fishers.

for weeks, collecting enough acorns to last through the year. Ohlone (oh-LONE-ee) families often had their own tree groves. Relatives from several nearby villages gathered in a family grove to harvest acorns there. In most cultures, men and women worked together to knock acorns from trees and pick them up off the ground. Women carried the acorns back to the village and prepared food from them. A celebration followed. People feasted, danced, and played games.

Several times a year, communities came together for ceremonies and councils. People called on the spirits to ask for help or to give thanks for a good harvest. In the spring, mountain-dwelling Maidu (MY-doo) communities held a thanksgiving ceremony called the bear dance. Every autumn,

MAIDU ACORN SONG

These traditional words are still sung during the acorn harvest, the biggest Maidu festival of the year:

Hu'-tim yo'-kim koi-o-di'.
The acorns come down from heaven.
Wi'-hi-yan'-ning koi-o-di'.
I plant the short acorns in the valley.
Lo'-whi yan'-ning koi-o-di'.
I plant the long acorns in the valley.
Yo-ho' nai-ni, hal-u'-dom yo nai, yo-ho' nainim'.
I sprout, I, the black acorn, sprout. I sprout.

northwestern groups—the Hupa, the Karuk, the Tolowa, the Wiyot, and the Yurok—held a huge World Renewal Ceremony. People danced and sang to pray for safety from events such as earthquakes, floods, or a poor salmon run. These gatherings helped native peoples strengthen community ties, express their beliefs, and pass on traditions.

CHAPTER 3

ART, MUSIC, AND DANCE

Early California Indians were expert craftspeople. Many of the objects they made had practical uses. But these objects could also be works of art.

Each California cultural group had distinctive artistic styles and skills. These cultures also had strong musical traditions. Song and dance helped communities remember their histories and connect with the spirit world. Many of these customs have been passed down to modern California Indians.

The Pomo Indians used this style of basket for cooking.

Crafts

Long ago, California Indians made baskets to carry seeds, plants, and water. Baskets were also used for cooking and storing food or medicine. Over the years,

BASKET MATERIALS USED BY CALIFORNIA PEOPLES

CULTURAL GROUP	TRADITIONAL BASKET MATERIALS
Luiseño	Coiled grass
Miwok	Coiled willow branches, sedge root, redbud bark, feathers, shells
Pomo	Blue jay, woodpecker, and quail feathers beads made from clamshells
Hupa, Karuk, and Yurok	Bark from alder trees, ferns, grasses, hazel and willow shoots, thin milkweed fibers made into cords

the baskets evolved into works of art. Basket makers decorated their work with designs and symbols, including trees, snakes, deer, mountains, and people holding hands. They added elements from nature, such as clamshell beads, abalone, or porcupine quills. Pomo baskets were often decorated with feathers, shells, and beads. Cahuilla and Yurok women wore basket hats made of twined grasses. Baskets were also given as gifts. Each basket maker used unique materials and patterns. So people could tell who had made a basket simply by looking at it.

Basketmaking was only one of the many crafts California Indians mastered. The Mojave sculpted clay dolls for children.

They decorated the dolls to look like people, with human hair. The Chumash carved animal figures from soapstone.

Jewelry

In many California groups, both men and women wore jewelry. Jewelry was a sign of wealth. It could also be used as money. The Maidu used shells and animal bones for their necklaces and earrings. They often added feathers for extra decoration. Luiseño men sometimes hung bear claws or deer hooves on necklaces, and they wove human hair into bracelets and anklets. Among coastal groups such as the Chumash, shells were made into hair decorations, beads, and necklaces. The Chumash also carved soapstone into earrings, nose rings, and necklaces.

Jewelry was a sign of wealth for California Indians. The necklaces shown here are made of shells, a common material in jewelry making.

BASKET WEAVER EVA SALAZAR

Eva Salazar has been weaving baskets like this one for most of her life.

Eva Salazar of the Kumeyaay has been weaving coiled baskets since she was seven years old. She learned from her mother and her aunt. She uses various native plants, including deer grass, juncus, sumac, yucca, and willow. She teaches her skills to other Kumeyaay tribal members and shows her work in museums.

Music and Dance

Music and dance were essential parts of life for California Indians. People danced at family and community gatherings. There were dances for the seasons, to honor ancestors, and to heal the sick. For groups that held World Renewal Ceremonies, including the Yurok, the Hupa, and the Karuk, two important dances are the white deerskin dance and the jump dance. The Hupa believed these dances could offer protection and good fortune. They danced not just for themselves but for everyone in the world.

At dances and other gatherings, people played flutes made from wood or from the bones of birds. The Hupa carved whistles

California Indians commonly played flutes at dances and celebrations. Some flutes were carved from wood or bone.

from wood or animal bone. The Maidu used hollow logs as drums. Across the region, rattles were far more common than drums. Rattles were made from many materials, including cocoons and turtle shells. Groups as far apart as the Tolowa and the Kumeyaay made instruments out of deer hooves. The Kumeyaay made deer hoof rattles joined to wooden handles, which they used at funerals. Central groups such as the Miwok and the Yokut made rattles called clapper sticks. A craftsperson started with a plank of wood about 2 feet (0.6 m) long and split it halfway through, leaving a handle. When the clapper was shaken, it made a sound and kept the rhythm for the dancers.

Songs were sung at ceremonies, festivals, and other gatherings. The Mojave performed songs to cure illness, honor the dead, and celebrate. People often sang more than one hundred songs in a night, with rattles and sticks to keep the rhythm.

Many native Californians sang bird songs. These songs told the history of a people from the point of view of birds. Cahuilla bird song ceremonies could last for days. Among the Kumeyaay, men sang the songs and kept the rhythm using gourd rattles filled with seeds. Women performed traditional dances called bird dances.

This instrumental rattle is made from deer hooves.

CHAPTER 4

CHANGES AND
CHALLENGES

In 1542, Europeans first arrived in California. A Spanish explorer named Juan Cabrillo sailed north from Mexico and landed in what is now the San Diego area. Cabrillo named it Alta California, which means "Upper California." (The name California comes from a fictional island in a Spanish novel.) Eventually, people simply called it California.

More Europeans arrived over the next few hundred years. Sir Francis Drake, an English explorer, came to the present-day San Francisco area in 1579. Russian traders began traveling to California from the north in the 1700s.

Spanish Missions

At first, no Europeans tried to establish settlements. For two hundred years, they came and went. They did some trading with California peoples but did not threaten their lands or ways of life. That began to change in 1769, when the first Spanish mission was established in San Diego. Spain did not want Great Britain or Russia to claim California as a colony. So Spain built missions and brought in Catholic missionaries to keep the area under Spanish control. They also moved in cattle, pigs, and crops from overseas.

The Spanish priests could not build the missions or take care of the animals and crops by themselves. They decided to use the local native peoples for labor. Missionaries offered California Indians beads, food, and clothing to encourage them to visit the missions. Once California Indians arrived at the missions, many were forced to stay and work. They were not allowed to leave. Women sewed, cooked, gardened, and made soaps and candles. Men were taught to farm instead of hunt, gather, and fish. These groups are often called Mission Indians. They include coastal groups such as the Cahuilla, the Chumash, the Kumeyaay, the Luiseño, the Serrano, and the Tongva.

The missionaries wanted California Indians to believe in

Spain built missions, such as Santa Clara de Asís (*above*), to try to keep California under its control.

Catholicism instead of their native religions. People who lived at missions were not allowed to practice their traditional beliefs or even to eat the food they were used to. Their children were not allowed to speak their native languages.

In 1775, the Kumeyaay rebelled and burned down Mission San Diego, but the mission was quickly rebuilt. Over the next half century, twenty-one missions were built along the coast. Military forts called presidios were built to protect the missions. Villages, farms, and ranchos—farms that raised animals—sprouted up all around the protected areas.

More Changes

In 1821, the Mexican people won their independence from Spanish rule. Alta California belonged to Mexico, and the Mexican government gave all the land to Mexicans. They told California Indians they were free to leave the missions. But

This illustration shows a presidio near San Francisco in 1822.

POPULATIONS OF CALIFORNIA INDIAN GROUPS

CULTURAL GROUP	ESTIMATED POPULATION IN 1770	POPULATION IN 1910	POPULATION IN 2015
Miwok	9,000	670	3,500
Chumash	10,000	74	213
Yurok	2,500	700	3,500
Hupa	1,000	500	2,600

most had no homeland left, and they had no money. All they could do was go to work on the ranchos, just as they had at the missions. By then, many native Californians had begun to die from European diseases such as malaria and smallpox.

The United States took over the area when they won the Mexican-American War in 1848. That year, gold was discovered in the mountains near present-day Sacramento. The 1849 gold rush brought hundreds of thousands of people to California in search of gold. The newcomers pushed California Indians off their lands and killed them if they refused to move.

Many people flocked to California to search for gold in 1849.

KINTPUASH

In 1873, the Modoc leader Kintpuash resisted the US government's efforts to move his people off their lands. While Kintpuash tried to negotiate with US officials, a small group of his men killed some European newcomers. Kintpuash was angry at his men but refused to turn them over to the United States. With his sister's help, he wrote a letter in English to US officials.

Kintpuash, chief of the Modoc Nation of California and Oregon

Let everything be wiped out, washed out, and let there be no more blood. . . . I have got but a few men and I don't see how I can give them up. Will [the US government] give up their people who murdered my people while they were asleep? I never asked for the people who murdered my people. . . . I could give up my horse . . . and wouldn't cry about it, but if I gave up my men I would have to cry about it.

Later that year, Kintpuash was captured and killed by the US Army. Most of the Modoc were forced onto reservations soon afterward.

When they lost their land, California Indians lost many of their old ways. Entire nations died from starvation and disease. Some joined other American Indian tribes.

Small groups of California Indians fought to keep what was left of their homelands. But California Indians were outnumbered by the military forces. They lost their homelands and were forced onto reservations. In 1872, for instance, the Modoc went to war against the United States. They were defeated and sent to reservations in Oregon and Oklahoma.

By 1900, the population had dropped from hundreds of thousands of California Indians to no more than eighteen thousand. Many villages had become graveyards. Although some groups are gone forever, others found ways to survive into the modern world.

CHAPTER 5

PASSING ON TRADITIONS

After centuries of turmoil, California Indians **endure.** They still fight against prejudice. Many live in poverty. But with more than one hundred Californian nations recognized by the US government, more native people live in California than in any other state.

Many California Indians keep their customs and traditional beliefs alive. Some study the languages of their ancestors. Some learn to make baskets. They often dance or play music in ceremonies.

California Indians are citizens of the United States. They are members of their own nations as well. Their laws are separate from US laws, and most groups have their own constitutions. Some have their own police forces and firefighting services.

Reservations and rancherias serve as headquarters for California nations. These small areas of land were set aside for American Indians to live separately from other Americans. They are called reservations if they are south of Los Angeles and called rancherias north of Los Angeles.

Reservations and rancherias have their own governments.

The Cahuilla have a committee of five people who listen to the whole nation before making a decision. Most nations have similar leadership councils. For instance, the Cahuilla Nation has nine reservations, each with its own council. The council of the Tuolumne Rancheria, a Miwok community, sometimes still meets in the local roundhouse.

Old and New Ways of Life

California Indians often have trouble finding jobs on reservations. Many California Indians move to cities to work. But nations have created businesses on their reservations. One Luiseño group planted orchards on its reservation and supplies oranges, lemons, and avocados to markets and grocery stores across the country. Another group runs a campground on its reservation near San Diego.

Some native communities welcome tourists, who spend money to camp or buy arts and crafts. Many nations educate visitors—and nation members—about their culture and history. In 2000, the Kumeyaay community opened the Barona Cultural Center and Museum, which focuses on American Indian history. Classes at the museum teach skills such as basket weaving, pottery, and storytelling.

The Cahuilla continue to guard the

Basket weaving has been a widely practiced art among California Indians for many years. This photo shows a modern basket in progress.

canyons where they lived long ago. They also work to protect the local water, plants, and animals such as bighorn sheep. They helped create the Santa Rosa and San Jacinto Mountains National Monument, a protected wilderness area.

The Hupa have always fished as part of their way of life. They own hatcheries, which protect young fish after they hatch from eggs. The fish are released into streams and rivers. When the fish grow large enough, they are sold to markets. The Yurok also depend on fishing and work to protect the Klamath River.

Among central groups such as the Pomo, basket makers still practice their art. However, in many areas, pesticides have made local plants unsafe to use. When weavers make baskets, they run the grasses through their mouths to soften them. These grasses have dangerous chemicals on them.

An organization called the California Indian Basketweavers Association promotes traditional basketmaking. It also aims to protect traditional lands and resources so that craftspeople can continue their work there. Annual gatherings give people a chance to share their skills.

Continuing Ceremonies

Many traditional California Indian ceremonies still take place. The Hupa and the Yurok continue the jump dance and the white deerskin dance. The Maidu host a yearly bear dance. Yokut residents of the Santa Rosa Rancheria hold a renewal celebration every March 1.

The Cahuilla, Kumeyaay, Luiseño, and others continue their traditions of bird singing and bird dancing. The Miwok Big Time Festival is held during the acorn harvest every fall. Visitors watch the dances and learn about Miwok traditions. The Wiyot Nation revived an annual practice that had been lost for many years. In

California Indians continue to gather every fall for the Miwok Big Time Festival, which takes place during the acorn harvest. In this photo, a group of Miwok men roast deer meat in a traditional earth oven.

2014, they held their first World Renewal Ceremony since 1860.

California Indian cultures have never stood still. Early peoples in the region constantly adapted to their environments. They traded with one another, sharing materials and customs. But even with many changes over the years, these peoples preserved their unique ways of life. Modern California Indians continue to honor ancient traditions and find new ways to express their cultures.

NOTABLE CALIFORNIA INDIANS

Rick Bartow (Wiyot and Yurok)

is a painter, printmaker, and sculptor. His work is in museum collections across the United States, including the National Museum of the American Indian in Washington, DC. He bases much of his work on stories and spirituality from his California Indian heritage.

Cynthia Gomez (Miwok)

is a lawyer who promotes American Indian causes in California. She served as chief justice of her community's tribal court. In 2010, she became the tribal adviser to California's governor, Jerry Brown. Her job is to help the California state government communicate and work with American Indian nations.

Naomi Lang (Karuk)

is a champion ice dancer. In 2002, she became the first American Indian female athlete to compete in the Olympic Games. Since then, she has performed professionally around the world. She is also an ice dancing coach.

Ernest Siva (Cahuilla and Serrano)

is a storyteller and musician. He is also the tribal historian and cultural adviser for the Morongo Band of Mission Indians. He founded the Dorothy Ramon Learning Center, named after the last native speaker of the Serrano language. The learning center works to preserve the Southern California Indian cultures, languages, history, and traditional arts.

Timeline

Each California Indian culture had its own way of recording history. This timeline is based on the Gregorian calendar, which Europeans brought to North America.

1542: Juan Rodriguez Cabrillo sails from Mexico to present-day San Diego.

1769: A Spanish missionary founds the first Catholic mission in California.

1775: California Indians destroy Mission San Diego.

1821: Mexico wins independence and takes over Alta California.

1849: The California gold rush begins.

1872–1873 The Modoc War takes place.

1991: The California Indian Basketweavers Association is founded.

2000: The Kumeyaay open the Barona Cultural Center and Museum.

2014: The Wiyot Nation holds its first World Renewal Ceremony since 1860.

Glossary

balsa: a bundle of cattails, tule, or other brush tied together to make a raft

breechcloth: a piece of leather tucked between the legs and held in place with a belt

cultural group: a group of people that shares many traits, including a language and ways of life, but not necessarily a government

dentalia: small mollusk shells used for trade and decoration

empire: a group of nations or regions controlled by one ruler or government

mission: a church-based headquarters for religious work

missionary: a religious worker who wants others to follow his or her religion

nation: a group of people that shares a language, culture, and governing system

obsidian: hard, glassy rock formed by molten lava

peoples: nations or cultural groups

prejudice: an unfair dislike of a person or group

presidio: a fort built for the military to protect an area

rancheria: a Spanish term for a small California Indian settlement, similar to a reservation

rancho: a large farm used for raising animals in Spanish-controlled California

reservation: an area of land set aside by the US government for the use of American Indians

self-governing: not controlled by an outside group or person

soapstone: a soft, smooth rock

thrive: to grow strong

tule: a type of grass that grows in wetlands, used for weaving baskets, mats, and roofs

Source Notes

25 Victor King Chesnut, *Plants Used by the Indians of Mendocino County, California* (Washington, DC: Government Printing Office, 1902), 341.

36 Roger M. Carpenter, *American Indian History Day by Day: A Reference Guide to Events* (Santa Barbara, CA: Greenwood, 2012), 98.

Selected Bibliography

Fagan, Brian M. *The First North Americans.* New York: Thames and Hudson, 2000.

Hoffman, Geralyn Marie, and Lynn H. Gamble. "A Teacher's Guide to Historical and Contemporary Kumeyaay Culture." Institute for Regional Studies of the Californias, San Diego State University. Accessed May 15, 2015. https://www.mtrp.org/assets/files/KumeyaayGuide.pdf.

Jennings, Francis. *The Founders of America: From the Earliest Migrations to the Present.* New York: W. W. Norton, 1993.

Minor, Marz, and Nono Minor. *The American Indian Craft Book.* Lincoln: University of Nebraska Press, 1978.

Pritzker, Barry. *A Native American Encyclopedia: History, Culture, and Peoples.* New York: Oxford University Press, 2000.

Treuer, Anton, ed. *Indian Nations of North America.* Washington, DC: National Geographic Society, 2013.

White, W. E. *History-Social Science for California.* Glenview, IL: Pearson Education, 2006.

Further Information

California Indians: Making a Difference
http://www.californiamuseum.org/california-indians-making-difference
This section of the California Museum's website gives a preview of the museum's exhibit on California Indians. Watch videos to hear native Californians talk about their peoples' histories and cultures.

Chumash: Play a Traditional Dice Game
http://www.nps.gov/samo/learn/kidsyouth/playpi.htm
Learn how to play the traditional Chumash dice game of *pi* (PUH) on this National Park Service website.

Elliott, Eric. *Dear Miss Karana*. Berkeley, CA: Heyday, 2016.
In this short chapter book, a Luiseño girl named Tishmal decides to translate the lyrics of an old song. The song was sung in the 1800s by the last speaker of a lost California Indian language. But that language is similar to the Luiseño language. Can Tishmal use her own cultural roots to discover the song's meaning?

Gimpel, Diane Marczely. *A Timeline History of Early American Indian Peoples*. Minneapolis: Lerner Publication, 2015. Learn about early nations from all around the future United States.

Tieck, Sarah. *Chumash*. Edina, MN: Abdo, 2015. Find out more about California's Chumash people and their ways of life.

Index

Photo Acknowledgments

The images in this book are used with the permission of: © iStockphoto.com/Bastar (paper background); © lienkie/123RF.com (tanned hide background); © iStockphoto.com/datmore, pp. 2–3; © Laura Westlund/Independent Picture Service, pp. 4, 6; © iStockphoto.com/digital94086, p. 7; © Marilyn Angel Wynn/Nativestock.com, pp. 11, 15, 21, 26, 28, 29, 30, 39, 41; © Kip Evans/Alamy, p. 13; © Drow_male/Wikimedia Commons (CC BY-SA 3.0), p. 16; Courtesy of the Phoebe A. Hearst Museum of Anthropology and the Regents of the University of California — pp. 18 (1-11033a,b), 22 (1-2834), 31 (1-2459); © Thomas Kitchin & Victoria Hurst/First Light/Getty Images, p. 24; © Nancy Nehring/E+/Getty Images, p. 33; © De Agostini Picture Library/G. Dagli Orti/Bridgeman Images, p. 34; © Peter Essick/Aurora Creative/Getty Images, p. 35; © JT VintageArt Resource, NY, p. 36.

Font cover: © Dan Schreiber/Shutterstock.com.